Spiritual Dynamics:
Understanding the Laws That Govern the Spiritual Realm

By

Rev. Dr. Rafielle E. Usher

Copyright © 2010

Table of Contents

Preface

The reason I developed this teaching on Spiritual Dynamics was to offer an alternative explanation for the supernatural occurrences that many believers experience. Often, believers are perplexed by the supernatural; they either do not understand it and seek more knowledge, or they choose to avoid it altogether.

Unfortunately, in their quest for understanding, believers sometimes encounter teachings that are not necessarily biblical. Many sources are doctrinally unsound or outright unbiblical. Some individuals turn to old-school charismatic teachings as a trusted source, not realizing that many of these teachings are false and border on heresy. Often, these teachings on the supernatural drift away from Scripture, relying instead on anecdotal personal experiences.

Then there are those who simply avoid the topic altogether. This avoidance is also unhealthy, as it causes believers to miss out on vital insights that could aid them during times of hardship.

As you progress through this study, you will notice that I have structured the teachings to provide scriptural explanations within their proper context. Of course, no teaching is absolutely perfect. However, my goal is to at least offer you an alternative perspective that is both valid and more aligned with biblical truth than the teachings currently available.

Chapter 1

Introduction to Spiritual Dynamics

Spiritual Dynamics refers to the laws and order that govern the spiritual realm in relation to the natural world. God has instituted these laws to ensure balance and protection for His creation. These principles guide human interaction with supernatural forces and provide a framework for understanding spiritual authority. While scripture does not explicitly define these laws, the evidence of their existence can be seen throughout the biblical narrative. Understanding these principles allows believers to navigate spiritual warfare with confidence, recognizing their authority in Christ.

Before delving into the four eras of spiritual dynamics, it is essential to establish a foundational understanding of why these eras exist and how they have shaped the spiritual and natural realms. The spiritual realm operates according to divine laws and order, much like the natural world follows physical laws such as gravity and motion. Without this divine structure, chaos would reign, and the balance between the seen and unseen worlds would be disrupted. The changes in spiritual dynamics over time reflect God's interaction with humanity and the shifting boundaries between the spiritual and natural realms.

Each era of spiritual dynamics reveals a unique period in which God's interaction with humanity and the influence of supernatural forces varied. These changes were not random but were a response to significant events, including the Fall, the Flood, the coming of Christ, and His ascension. By examining these transitions, we gain insight into how spiritual warfare operates today and what authority believers hold in the present age. Understanding the progression of these eras helps us comprehend why certain spiritual interactions—such as angelic visitations, demonic manifestations, and divine interventions—were more prevalent in one era than another. This knowledge equips believers with a historical and theological framework for navigating their faith and spiritual battles today.

Chapter 2

The Four Eras of Spiritual Dynamics

There are four distinct eras of spiritual dynamics, each characterized by unique interactions between the spiritual and natural realm. It is expected that you will see these interactions and gain a better understanding of how they affected mankind throughout each of the four eras.

The first era, from Creation to the Fall, was marked by mankind's ability to communicate directly with God, interact with animals on a profound level, and perceive the spiritual realm. During this time, Satan could take on the physical form of animals. Humans had the ability to see the face of God and walk in His presence, as seen in Genesis 3:8, where Adam and Eve heard the sound of God walking in the garden. This level of direct communion with God highlights the unique spiritual environment of this era.

Additionally, humans possessed the extraordinary ability to converse with animals, as evidenced in Genesis 3:1-2, where Eve engages in dialogue with the serpent. This interaction indicates a profound connection between humanity and creation, enabling a deeper comprehension of the natural world. Notably, Eve's lack of surprise at encountering a talking animal suggests that such occurrences were familiar to her. It is also worthy to note that during this time, it seems Satan himself could only manifest through the form of an animal. Genesis 3:1 depicts Satan taking on the form of a serpent to deceive Eve, illustrating how spiritual beings interacted with the physical realm under specific limitations.

Moreover, heavenly angels had access to the physical world under God's command, as seen in Genesis 3:24, where cherubim were stationed at the entrance to the Garden of Eden to guard the way to the tree of life. This indicates that while angelic beings could operate in the natural world, their actions were strictly governed by God's Divine authority. These characteristics of the first era demonstrate a time when the spiritual and natural realms coexisted in a way that was far more direct and tangible than in later eras.

The second era, from the Fall to the Great Flood, saw a shift in dynamics where mankind lost the ability to see God, yet still retained some communication with the spiritual realm. Humans could no longer see the face of God, though they were still able to walk with Him in faith, as recorded in Genesis 5:22, 5:24, and 6:9. This signifies a change in how God's divine presence was perceived. Despite this loss, humans still retained the ability to communicate with animals, as seen in Genesis 7:9, indicating a lingering connection between mankind and the rest of creation. However, demonic activity increased during this era. Demons gained the ability to physically interact in the natural realm without restriction, even taking human form and procreating with women, as stated in Genesis 6:2 and 6:4. This period saw a significant corruption of both human and spiritual interactions. Heavenly angels still had access to the physical realm, but only under the direct orders of God, as demonstrated in their role surrounding the events of the great flood.

The third era, from the Flood to the Ascension of Christ, introduced further restrictions on demonic beings. While God occasionally revealed His face to certain individuals, as in Exodus 33:11, the widespread ability to see God was not restored. The ability to speak with animals was lost entirely, as demonstrated in

Numbers 22:28-30, where Balaam's donkey speaking was a unique and miraculous event rather than a normal occurrence. No other scriptures contradict this change. Demons lost their ability to physically interact in the natural realm unless they possessed a physical body, marking a significant limitation compared to previous eras. There are no scriptures indicating that demons could act independently in the physical world beyond possession. Additionally, angels were now assigned the role of delivering answers to prayers, as seen in Daniel 10:13, further demonstrating the increasing mediation between the spiritual and natural realms.

The fourth and final era, from ascension to Christ's Return, is the era we currently live in. This period is defined by the authority given to believers through Jesus Christ. Unlike in previous eras, demons no longer have free reign but must gain permission through human consent. Understanding the distinctions between these eras is crucial in comprehending how spiritual warfare operates today.

Chapter 3

The Four Eras of Spiritual Authority Over the Earth

From the very beginning, God established a divine order of authority over the earth, entrusting mankind with dominion under His sovereign rule. However, this authority was not static but shifted throughout history due to mankind's choices, rebellion, and God's redemptive plan. Scripture reveals a progression of four distinct spiritual eras: from creation to the fall of man, from the fall of man to the flood, from the flood to the ascension of Christ, and from the ascension of Christ to His return.

Each of these transitions reflects the broader spiritual battle between God's kingdom and the forces of darkness. Understanding these shifts is essential for recognizing the believer's rightful authority in Christ and the ongoing struggle between God's sovereignty and Satan's temporary dominion over the unredeemed world. Through a biblical lens, this section explores these four eras, examining how divine authority has been established, lost, and ultimately restored through Christ Jesus.

First Era: Creation to the Fall

In the beginning, God established the order of spiritual authority with Himself as supreme, man as His representative over creation, and Satan in subjection to mankind. This divine order is clearly stated in Genesis 1:26 (KJV): "And God said, Let us make man in our image, after our likeness: and let them have dominion over the fish of the sea, and over the fowl of the air, and over the cattle, and over all the earth, and over every creeping thing that creepeth upon the earth."

God's intent was for man to govern the earth as a steward under His authority, reflecting His righteousness, wisdom, and justice. This dominion included tending to the land (Genesis 2:15) and exercising righteous rule over creation. It was a theocratic hierarchy where God reigned over man, and man, in turn, had authority over the earth, including dominion over Satan. Since man was created in God's image, his rulership was to reflect God's character, meaning he was to subdue and maintain the earth in accordance with God's will (Psalm 8:6: "Thou madest him to have dominion over the works of thy hands; thou hast put all things under his feet.").

Second Era: The Fall to the Flood

The order of spiritual authority was drastically altered when Adam and Eve sinned. Genesis 3:13 (KJV) states, "And the Lord God said unto the woman, What is this that thou hast done? And the woman said, The serpent beguiled me, and I did eat." The deception by Satan led to man's disobedience, causing humanity to forfeit its God-given authority over the earth. As a result, Satan usurped dominion, becoming the ruling spiritual power over fallen mankind and the earth.

This period saw great corruption and violence, including fallen angels engaging in forbidden acts with human women, resulting in the Nephilim (Genesis 6:4). The Bible describes this era as filled with extreme wickedness and violence (Genesis 6:5, 11). Because man surrendered his authority, the spiritual hierarchy shifted: God remained supreme, but Satan became the ruler over mankind and the earth, bringing chaos and rebellion against God's order.

Third Era: The Flood to the Ascension of Christ

As wickedness increased, God reasserted His sovereign authority by judging the earth through the flood. Genesis 6:6 (KJV) states, "And it repented the Lord that he had made man on the earth, and it grieved him at his heart." The word "repented" in this context does not mean God made a mistake but rather signifies a change in divine action—God was reclaiming authority over the earth by executing judgment upon all except Noah and his family.

Following the flood, the order of spiritual authority was restructured. God was now directly ruling over the earth again, but due to mankind's fallen nature, Satan still held dominion over unredeemed individuals. This is why 2 Corinthians 4:4 (KJV) states, "In whom the god of this world hath blinded the minds of them which believe not, lest the light of the glorious gospel of Christ, who is the image of God, should shine unto them." Here, "the god of this world" refers to Satan, highlighting his continued influence over humanity outside of God's covenant.

Fourth Era: The Ascension of Christ to His Return (Present Day)

With the coming of Christ and His redemptive work, the spiritual authority structure was once again transformed. Through His victory over sin and death, Jesus restored mankind's rightful position of authority in the kingdom of God. Matthew 28:18 (KJV) declares, "And Jesus came and spake unto them, saying, All power is given unto me in heaven and in earth." This statement affirms Christ's supreme authority over all creation, which He shares with those who believe in Him.

Believers are now spiritually positioned with Christ. Ephesians 2:6 (KJV) confirms this truth: "And hath raised us up together, and made us sit together in heavenly places in Christ Jesus." This means that through faith in Christ, believers have regained the authority that was lost in the Garden of Eden, being seated with Christ in a place of spiritual dominion. Furthermore, Philippians 2:9-10 (KJV) emphasizes Christ's exalted status: "Wherefore God also hath highly exalted him, and given him a name which is above every name: That at the name of Jesus every knee should bow, of things in heaven, and things in earth, and things under the earth."

However, 2 Corinthians 4:4 reminds us that Satan still holds sway over those who reject Christ, acting as the "god of this world" to the unbelieving. We must also take into account that Ephesians Chapter 6 tells us that, as Christians, we are at war with the hierarchical structure that Satan has put in place over the earth. As believers, we have been given armor to protect us from the enemy; however, non-believers do not have this protection and are therefore more easily subject to demonic influences. Therefore, while believers in Christ have spiritual authority over Satan, those outside of Christ remain under his dominion.

Never assume that Christians and nonbelievers are governed by the same authority structure—we are not. Remember Ephesians 2:6: "We are seated together with Christ in heavenly places." If we are seated in Christ, then we are also seated in heavenly places, "far above all principality and power and might and dominion, and every name that is named, not only in this age but also in that which is to come" (Ephesians 1:21). This means we are not under Satan's hierarchical structure; we are above it!

Chapter 4

The Four Laws that Govern the Spiritual Realm

Now that you have learned about the four eras, let's discuss the current era we are living in and the laws and authority under which we currently operate. Remember, the spiritual realm operates under specific laws that, though not explicitly stated in Scripture, are evident through biblical events and teachings. These laws govern the interaction between the natural and supernatural realms and reveal God's divine order. Christian evangelical theology affirms that the Bible provides sufficient revelation for understanding these spiritual dynamics. Through exegesis, believers can discern patterns in Scripture that outline the principles guiding spiritual warfare and divine authority. The following laws illustrate the biblical framework of spiritual dynamics and their implications for believers today.

Law #1: The Authority of Jesus Christ

The foremost spiritual law is the absolute authority of Jesus Christ over all creation. Matthew 28:18 declares, "All authority in heaven and on earth has been given to me." This authority extends over both the natural and spiritual realms, ensuring that nothing operates outside of Christ's dominion. Mark 1:27 highlights that even unclean spirits obey Jesus' command, demonstrating His supreme power over demonic forces. Additionally, Luke 8:25 affirms that even the elements of nature submit to His word. This law assures believers that Christ's authority is the foundation of all spiritual dynamics, and through Him, they possess dominion over spiritual adversaries. The implications of this law mean that every demonic force, every principality, and every power must bow to the name of Jesus, reinforcing the believer's victory through faith.

Law #2: No Spirit Can Override Human Free Will

Another fundamental law in spiritual dynamics is that no spirit, whether angelic or demonic, can override human free will. James 4:7 instructs believers to "Submit yourselves, then, to God. Resist the devil, and he will flee from you." This verse implies that the power to resist the enemy lies within an individual's decision to yield to God. I Timothy 4:1 further reinforces this principle, where the root word "ἀποστασία" (aposta) signifies a deliberate act of will, illustrating that spiritual deception occurs through human consent. Genesis 2 and 3 provide the first example of human free will, as Adam and Eve made the conscious choice to disobey God. Joshua 24:15 echoes this truth, urging people to "Choose this day whom you will serve." Even in cases of demonic possession, such as the man in Luke 8:30, the demons could not force him to flee from Jesus. Why didn't the demons simply take control of the man and make him run away? Because his free will remained intact. This demonstrates that demonic influence requires human cooperation for the demon to operate fully. The implications of this principle ensure that believers are never helpless against spiritual attacks; rather, they must actively resist and stand firm in their faith in Christ.

NOTE: Just as Satan deceived Eve, demons can trick you into doing things. If you do not willingly give Satan power over your will, then the only weapon he can use against you is the weapon of temptation, tricking you into doing something you do not want to do (1 Corinthians 10:13; James 1:13-14).

Law #3: The Power of Spoken Words

The third spiritual law concerns the authority of spoken words in shaping spiritual outcomes. Mark 11:23 states, "Truly I tell you, if anyone says to this mountain, 'Go, throw yourself into the sea,' and does not doubt in their heart but believes that what they say will happen, it will be done for them." This passage underscores the authoritative power of words in the spiritual realm. Romans 10:9 emphasizes the necessity of verbal confession for salvation, reinforcing the idea that spoken words have tangible spiritual consequences. Even when you are casting out demons, the bible teaches us to invoke the name of Jesus verbally. Additionally, in Luke 11:13 it teaches that receiving the Holy Spirit requires asking (speaking words), and Ephesians 3:20 reveals that God responds even to our thoughts. Since 90% of spiritual warfare occurs in the mind, as seen in Romans 7:23 and 8:5-7, maintaining control over one's thoughts and confessions is essential for spiritual victory. This law aligns with Proverbs 18:21, which declares that "Death and life are in the power of the tongue." The practical application of this law encourages believers to guard their speech and declare the truth of God's Word over their lives to enforce victory in spiritual battles.

Note: Let me be clear—our words do not have creative power. We are not God, and we cannot speak things into existence. Only God possesses the ability to create ex nihilo (out of nothing), as demonstrated in Genesis 1:3, where He said, *"Let there be light,"* and it was so. However, our words do have the power to influence ourselves, those around us, and the situations we encounter. Proverbs 18:21 affirms this truth: *"Death and life are in the power of the tongue, and those who love it will eat its fruit."* Our words are not creative forces but rather a physical expression of the thoughts in our hearts. As Luke 6:45 states, *"For out of the abundance of the heart his mouth speaks."*

When our words are used in prayer and under the authority of Christ, they become a tool that God uses to accomplish His will on earth and to make Himself known. James 5:16 emphasizes the power of righteous prayer, stating, *"The effective, fervent prayer of a righteous man avails much."* Likewise, Isaiah 55:11 reminds us that it is God's word—not ours—that carries divine power: *"So shall My word be that goes forth from My mouth; it shall not return to Me void, but it shall accomplish what I please."* Therefore, while our words do not create reality, they serve as instruments in the hands of God when spoken in faith, aligning with His divine purposes.

Law #4: Spirits Cannot Freely Interact in the Physical Realm Without a Physical Body

Another significant spiritual law is that spirits cannot freely operate in the natural realm without inhabiting a physical body. Throughout the New Testament, there is no record of spirits moving objects or engaging in physical acts unless they possess a living entity. Mark 5:1-13 provides a clear example of this principle, where demons had to enter a herd of pigs in order to continue their activity. Acts 19:14-16 further illustrates this law, showing that the possessed man, not the demons themselves, physically attacked the seven sons of Sceva. This passage confirms that spirits require a host to exert influence in the physical realm. If demons could independently act in the natural realm, they would not need human hosts or animals to carry out their will. Jude 1:6 affirms that fallen angels who left their proper domain were bound in chains, restricting their ability to operate in the physical world as they once did. Evidence for this is found in Jude 1:5, which explicitly states that these satanic angels lost the special powers they once had as archangels. This concept is reinforced by the Greek translation of the verse. The Greek text uses μή (mē), τηρέω (tēreō), and ἀρχή (archē)—Strong's Concordance numbers 5083 and 746—which collectively indicate that these angels *"did not keep"* or *"lost the abilities of arch."* This interpretation aligns with biblical theology, emphasizing that fallen angels no longer possess the unrestricted authority they once had. Instead, 2 Peter 2:4 further clarifies their fate: *"For if God did not spare the angels who sinned, but cast them down to hell and delivered them into chains of darkness, to be reserved for judgment."* This confirms that their former dominion has been stripped, and they now operate under certain limitations while awaiting divine judgment.

The implications of this law assure believers that demonic forces cannot directly harm them without special permission from God, as demonstrated in Revelation 9:4-5 (NKJV): "They were commanded not to harm the grass of the earth, or any green thing, or any tree, but only those men who do not have the seal of God on their foreheads. And they were not given authority to kill them, but to torment them for five months. Their torment was like the torment of a scorpion when it strikes a man." This passage clearly shows that even demonic forces operate within the boundaries set by God, reinforcing the truth that believers who are sealed by God remain under His divine protection. This emphasizes the importance of resisting temptation and remaining spiritually vigilant. However, the limitations placed on demons does not apply to angels under God's authority. In fact, numerous Scriptures affirm that God's angels have the ability to interact with the physical realm (John 5:4; Matthew 28:2; Acts 5:19; Acts 12:7).

Lets look back at the first era of spiritual dynamics, the Sons of God (fallen angels or demons) had the ability to take physical form and interact directly with humans—even to the extent of

17

reproducing with them (Genesis 6:1-4). However, after God saw the corruption this caused, He changed the order of spiritual interaction, preventing demons from physically manifesting in the natural world. From that moment on, Scripture never records demons having direct physical interactions with humans or objects unless they possessed a physical body.

The book of Job, often considered the oldest book in the Bible, provides insight into postdiluvian (post-flood) spiritual dynamics. Some scholars believe it was written before Moses composed Genesis. Since Genesis records events from the beginning of creation, it is plausible that the events in Job took place between the time period of Genesis chapter 10 and 11. During this postdiluvian era, Satan had lost the unique ability to freely operate within the physical, natural world. As recorded in Job 1:12, Satan needed permission from God to afflict Job physically. If the prediluvian (pre-flood) spiritual dynamics were still in effect, then Satan would not have needed to obtain God's permission to physically attack Job. Satan needing permission from God during the postdiluvian period is proof that demonic interaction in the physical realm had ended when God established new spiritual boundaries, as seen in Genesis 6:7, where God "repented that He had '*made*' them." The word "made" in Hebrew is עָשָׂה (ʿāśâ) means appointed, ordained, or instituted. This verse effectively means that God reversed His original appointment of man as the authority over the earth, and re-establishes His own authority over the earth.

This means that the spiritual dynamics in Job's time cannot be used to explain the dynamics of the post-Christ ascension era. After Christ's resurrection, spiritual warfare fundamentally changed, with demons being restricted to operating through human hosts rather than directly interacting with the material world.

The point that I want to drive home is this: If demons had free reign in the physical realm, they would not need to manipulate or possess humans. All they would need to do is simply pick up a knife and kill believers themselves. However, demons lack the ability to act physically on their own, which is why they seek to influence and manipulate human will to carry out their destructive intentions (John 8:44). This distinction reinforces the necessity of spiritual vigilance, as demons operate through deception and influence rather than direct physical action.

Remember, the spiritual realm operates under Divinely established laws that govern interactions between the supernatural and natural realm. These principles are both evident and applicable to believers today. Understanding these laws empowers believers to navigate spiritual warfare effectively, exercising authority through Jesus Christ, safeguarding their free will, speaking life through their words, and recognizing the limitations of demonic influence in the physical realm. By applying these biblical truths, believers can walk in spiritual victory and fulfill God's purpose for their lives.

Chapter 5

Understanding Spirits and Possession

In biblical language, the word "spirit" can refer to different concepts, making it necessary to distinguish between meanings. For example, in Matthew 14:26, the disciples saw Jesus walking on water and cried out in fear, thinking they had seen a ghost. The Greek word used here is φαντασμα (*phantasma*), meaning an apparition or phantom. In contrast, 2 Timothy 1:7 states, "For God has not given us a spirit (πνεῦμα, *pneuma*) of fear, but of power and of love and of a sound mind." Here, *pneuma* refers to a disposition or an inner spiritual condition. However, in Mark 5:2, where Jesus encounters the man possessed by demons, the word πνεύματι (*pneumati*) is used to describe an actual unclean spirit. Understanding these distinctions prevents misinterpretations when studying spiritual matters in Scripture.

This brings us to a critical question: Can a Christian be demon-possessed? The answer is an absolute no! Possession implies ownership, and the moment a person accepts Christ, He takes full ownership of their entire being. 1 Corinthians 6:19-20 declares, "Or do you not know that your body is the temple of the Holy Spirit who is in you, whom you have from God, and you are not your own? For you were bought at a price; therefore glorify God in your body and in your spirit, which are God's." Some claim that demons can inhabit areas of a Christian's life that have not been fully surrendered to God. However, there is no biblical justification for this belief—it is pure heresy. Romans 4:7-8 affirms, "Blessed are those whose lawless deeds are forgiven, and whose sins are covered; blessed is the man to whom the Lord shall not impute sin." Christ's atoning work covers all sins, including those unknown to us, and God has promised never to count them against us.

Some argue over semantics, asserting that Christians cannot be possessed but can be "demonized." However, any scholar trained in biblical hermeneutics knows that the Greek word δαιμονιζόμαι (*daimonizomai*)—which is used in Scripture—refers explicitly to demon possession. There is no distinction between possession and demonization in the original biblical texts. If a Christian cannot be possessed, then how do we biblically explain the demonic activity they sometimes experience? I have three answers.

The first answer is that while Christians cannot be demon-possessed, they can suffer demonic **affliction**. 1 Peter 5:8-9 warns believers, "Be sober, be vigilant; because your adversary the devil walks about like a roaring lion, seeking whom he may devour. Resist him, steadfast in the faith, knowing that the same sufferings are experienced by your brotherhood in the world." The Greek word used for "sufferings" here is παθημα (*pathema*), meaning external affliction, misfortune, or calamity. Many struggles believers face—whether in health, relationships, or circumstances—are spiritual attacks. However, deliverance comes through exercising spiritual authority in Christ. By calling on Jesus and walking in faith putting their trust in Him, believers can overcome these afflictions.

The second answer is buffeting. In 2 Corinthians 12:7, the Apostle Paul states, "And lest I should be exalted above measure by the abundance of the revelations, a thorn in the flesh was given to me, a messenger of Satan to buffet me, lest I be exalted above measure." In this passage, it does not specify who sent the messenger of Satan, but the messenger's job was to buffet Paul. The word buffet in Greek is κολαφίζω (kolaphizō), which literally means "to strike with the fist, to give a blow with the fist, to maltreat, and to treat with violence and contempt."

Paul confirms this as he continues his discourse in verses 9-10, saying, "Therefore, I take pleasure in infirmities, in reproaches, in needs, in persecutions, in distresses, for Christ's sake. For when I am weak, then I am strong." Here, we see three hints as to what the buffeting entailed. Paul mentions "weakness," "infirmities," "reproaches," "needs," "persecutions," and "distress." All of these illustrate demonic buffeting, which God allowed and used to strengthen Paul's dependence and trust in Him. God uses this same buffeting to teach believers to rely on His faithfulness rather than their own strength and wisdom.

As we review Paul's discourse, notice how he states in verse 8 that he pleaded with God to remove the buffeting, but God denied his request because Paul's suffering was part of God's eternal plan. This teaches us that sometimes Christians will be buffeted—not as a form of punishment, but as a demonstration of God's faithfulness in caring for us through hardship.

Think about it: there are people around you watching your life's story unfold. For some, you are the only Bible they will ever see. God's purpose for your suffering is to teach you how to be faithful when things get hard. However, being faithful does not mean faking that you are not suffering or hiding what you are feeling. The best witness to a lost and dying world is authenticity.

Be authentic in your walk with God as you endure buffeting. It is okay to feel angry, disappointed, confused, or even hurt by what you are going through. But the goal is always to return to the faithfulness of God. He knows what He is doing and why. We are not called to understand or explain why God does what He does—we are only called to walk by faith and proclaim His glory to a lost and dying world.

On a side note, imagine how the world would respond if they saw you endure buffeting while maintaining an authentic relationship with God. Can you picture how awe-inspiring that would be? Onlookers might say: "That person is going through hell, and yet they are still faithful to God. There must be something to this God thing after all!"

Try to understand that your suffering has a purpose—it has the potential to build the faith of those watching. Even though you are being buffeted, God will provide you with supernatural grace to endure it.

The third answer incorporates a broader theological perspective. Psalm 51:5 states, "Behold, I was brought forth in iniquity, and in sin my mother conceived me." This verse highlights the reality of humanity's sin nature from birth. Because we are born into sin, demonic forces have worked since our infancy to shape our thoughts, responses, and behaviors. This is a form of spiritual conditioning, not possession. Romans 12:2 provides the solution: "And do not be conformed to this world, but be transformed by the renewing of your mind, that you may prove what is that good and acceptable and perfect will of God." Likewise, 2 Corinthians 10:5 instructs believers to "cast down arguments and every high thing that exalts itself against the knowledge of God, bringing every thought into captivity to the obedience of Christ." The responsibility to renew the mind lies with the believer, as God has already given authority over demonic influences.

In review, there are three explanations for demonic activity in the life of a believer. The first is afflictions, which refer to misfortune or calamity. The second is buffeting, which includes "weakness," "infirmities," "reproaches," "needs," "persecutions," and "distress." The third is non-demonic sin nature, which refers to the normal human suffering that all mankind experiences.

Chapter 6

Casting Out Demons – Myths and Realities

Many misconceptions exist regarding deliverance from demonic oppression. Some false doctrines insist that in order to cast out demons, one must pray for extended hours daily, fast beforehand, or live a completely sinless life to be effective. These false doctrines also claim that failing to follow these prescribed steps will leave a person vulnerable to demonic attacks. However, 1 Peter 5:8 (NKJV) warns, "Be sober, be vigilant; because your adversary the devil walks about like a roaring lion, seeking whom he may devour." This verse makes it clear that Satan is always seeking to attack, regardless of whether one actively participates in deliverance ministry or not. Spiritual warfare is inevitable for all believers, but Philippians 2:10-11 assures us that at the name of Jesus, every knee must bow, and Satan has already been defeated.

Because of this, the idea that spiritual authority is earned through personal effort is fundamentally flawed. Many of these teachings are works-based doctrines rather than faith-based doctrines, placing unnecessary burdens on believers that Scripture does not support. Mark 16:17 (NKJV) states, "And these signs will follow those who believe: In My name they will cast out demons; they will speak with new tongues." Deliverance is not dependent on human effort but on Christ's authority alone. It is crucial to understand one fundamental truth: You are not the one casting out the demon—Jesus is the one doing the work! While prayer, fasting, and righteous living are essential in the Christian life, they should never be viewed as prerequisites for deliverance. Authority over demons comes through faith in Jesus, not through excessive preparation or human striving. Some misinterpret Ephesians 6:18, which speaks of "praying always," to mean that unceasing prayer is required to maintain spiritual authority. However, the Greek word kairos (καιρός), translated as "always," refers to specific appointed times, not a never-ending, uninterrupted act. This means that consistent prayer is important, but legalistic requirements for deliverance ministry are unbiblical.

In addition to placing unnecessary spiritual burdens on believers, many false teachings promote unbiblical methods for casting out demons. Some claim that drinking "anointing oil" or "holy water," inducing vomiting, blowing smoke into one's ears, or cracking joints to release spirits are necessary. Others insist that one must confess sins from past generations, fast excessively, or pray for prolonged hours before deliverance can take place. These man-made rituals have no biblical basis. Ezekiel 18:20 (NKJV) declares, "The son shall not bear the guilt of the father, nor the father bear the guilt of the son." Furthermore, 1 John 1:9 assures believers that God forgives sin when we confess directly to Him— without the need for extra rituals. True deliverance is not found in human traditions, but in the power and authority of Jesus Christ alone.

So, the question then arises: where does the notion or belief of preparation, such as excessive fasting and prayer, come from in relation to casting out demons? This belief stems from a Bible teaching found in Matthew 17:19-21: "Then the disciples came to Jesus privately and said, 'Why could we not cast it out?' So Jesus said to them, 'Because of your unbelief; for assuredly, I say to you, if you have faith as a mustard seed, you will say to this mountain, 'Move from here to there,' and it will move; and nothing will be impossible for you. However, this kind does not go out except by prayer and fasting.'"

One thing that people often forget when reading this story is that this incident happened before Jesus died on the cross and before the empowerment of the Holy Spirit. At that time, the disciples were still operating under the third-era laws of spiritual dynamics. It is crucial to note that Jesus did not declare, "All authority has been given to Me in heaven and on earth" until after His resurrection from the dead, as recorded in Matthew 28:18. You will never see anyone after the resurrection of Christ and Pentecost struggling to cast out demons. Remember, when Christ died, the Bible says in Ephesians 4:8-10: "Wherefore He says, 'Having ascended up on high, He has led captivity captive and has given gifts to men.' In saying, 'He ascended,' what does it mean but that He had also descended into the lower regions, the earth? He who descended is the one who also ascended far above all the heavens, that He might fill all things." This passage is often interpreted to mean that Christ went into Hell, took Satan's authority, and released those unjustly held captive by Satan. According to evangelical theology, this refers to those who died in the Old Testament as followers of God but had not yet had the opportunity to know Christ. The Bible confirms this in Revelation 1:18, where Jesus declares: "I am He who lives, and was dead, and behold, I am alive forevermore. Amen. And I have the keys of Hades and of Death." This provides proof that Christ took command and authority away from Satan and his demons.

Does all this mean that a person does not need to fast and pray? No, absolutely not. However, what I am saying is that fasting and prayer must never be engaged in as a form of works to earn the right to cast out demons or perform anything supernatural. The moment you step into works, you stop operating in faith, and we all know what happens when you stop operating in faith—nothing!

A true story illustrates this principle. While serving in the Mayan Zone, I trained numerous churches and pastors on spiritual dynamics. Some embraced the teaching, while others remained skeptical. One evening, after returning to the U.S., I received an urgent phone call from two pastors in the Mayan Zone. They had encountered a young girl they believed to be demon-possessed. Despite fasting, praying, and anointing her with oil, the demon would not leave. They asked me what to do.

I responded with a few questions. First, I asked, "Did you fast and pray before praying for her?" They answered, "Yes, but perhaps not long enough." I reminded them that Jesus only fasted once before beginning His ministry. Then I asked, "Did you use anointing oil?" They confirmed they had. "How many times did you invoke the name of Jesus?" "Many times," they replied. I then said, "If you've fasted, prayed, anointed with oil, and invoked Jesus' name without success, have you considered that this might not be a demon at all?"

I instructed them to pray for the girl's healing instead of deliverance. As I had taught them, not all healings are immediate. They agreed and went to pray for her healing. A few hours later, they called me back, overjoyed. "Pastor Rafa! You were right! When we prayed for her healing, she started improving, and now she is completely well!"

In this testimony, even though I was being a bit facetious, it underscores the importance of discernment. Not every struggle is demonic; some are physical, emotional, or psychological in nature.

Jesus did not use the same approach for every case. The key to victory lies in spiritual authority, biblical wisdom, discernment and faith in Christ's finished work. As Luke 10:19 declares, "Behold, I give you the authority to trample on serpents and scorpions, and over all the power of the enemy, and nothing shall by any means hurt you."

Chapter 7

Prayers: Myths and Realities

In this discussion, we will examine commonly held teachings about prayer and intercessory prayer, particularly misconceptions that have shaped the way many believers approach communication with God. One frequently cited passage is Daniel 10:13, where a spiritual force hindered Daniel's prayers. However, this example cannot be used to explain post-resurrection spiritual dynamics. Daniel's experience occurred under the Old Covenant, where God's presence was distant, and angelic messengers played a significant role in delivering divine responses. However, under the New Covenant, we, as followers of Christ, have direct access to God through Jesus. When Christ died, the veil of the temple was torn in two (Matthew 27:51), signifying that God's presence is no longer restricted to a temple but dwells among us and within us. Hebrews 4:16 (NKJV) declares, "Let us therefore come boldly to the throne of grace, that we may obtain mercy and find grace to help in time of need." This means that no demon can stop, hinder, or delay our prayers, as we now have unrestricted access to God.

One common myth is that Satan can stop, hinder, or delay our prayers. However, 1 John 5:15 (NKJV) assures us, "And if we know that He hears us, whatever we ask, we know that we have the petitions that we have asked of Him." If God hears our prayers and grants them according to His will, no spiritual force can interfere. Another misconception is that praying for hours or days increases the likelihood of receiving an answer. While persistent prayer keeps the believer's mind focused on Jesus and strengthens faith, it is not a bargaining tool to force God's hand. James 5:16 (NKJV)

33

states, "The effective, fervent prayer of a righteous man avails much." The power of prayer is in faith, not in its duration.

Some believe that praying aloud allows Satan to hear and stop their prayers. However, nowhere in Scripture does it say that the devil has the authority to block communication between a believer and God. Romans 8:26-27 teaches that the Holy Spirit intercedes for us, meaning our prayers are strengthened by divine power, not hindered by demonic forces. Another false teaching is that angels deliver answered prayers from Heaven. This idea is rooted in Old Testament examples, but under the New Covenant, prayers are answered directly by God. Matthew 7:7 (NKJV) reminds us, "Ask, and it will be given to you; seek, and you will find; knock, and it will be opened to you." Lastly, some believe that prayer can force another person to do something against their will, but God does not override human free will. He influences hearts through His Spirit, but He does not manipulate or coerce.

While there are myths about prayer, the Bible provides hard truths that affirm our direct and unhindered connection to God. First, He always hears us (1 John 5:15), and the only thing that hinders prayer is unresolved strife in personal relationships. 1 Peter 3:7 (NKJV) warns husbands, "Husbands, likewise, dwell with them with understanding, giving honor to the wife, as to the weaker vessel, and as being heirs together of the grace of life, that your prayers may not be hindered." Similarly, Matthew 5:23-24 teaches that before presenting an offering, a believer must first be reconciled to a brother.

We also have various types of prayer that are effective when exercised through faith. James 5:15 (NKJV) states, "And the prayer of faith will save the sick, and the Lord will raise him up." This prayer of faith relies on trust in God's ability to heal and deliver.

Additionally, Matthew 18:19 (NKJV) emphasizes the prayer of agreement, saying, "Again I say to you that if two of you agree on earth concerning anything that they ask, it will be done for them by My Father in heaven." Beyond this, we have unlimited access to God's throne (Hebrews 4:16) and the assurance that we are more than conquerors in Christ (Romans 8:37).

In summary, prayer is a direct line of communication with God that cannot be hindered by Satan, angels, or external forces. The effectiveness of prayer is rooted in faith, obedience, and a right relationship with God, not in religious rituals or extended duration. As believers, we must reject false doctrines and stand on the biblical truth that our prayers reach God instantly and are answered according to His will and in His timing.

Chapter 8

Prayers Over Cities and Locales

The spiritual realm operates within a hierarchical structure, as outlined in Ephesians 6:12 (NKJV): "For we do not wrestle against flesh and blood, but against principalities, against powers, against the rulers of the darkness of this age, against spiritual hosts of wickedness in the heavenly places." While this verse confirms the existence of demonic hierarchies, it is crucial to understand that as believers in Christ, we are positioned above all these spiritual forces. Ephesians 1:20-22 (NKJV) declares, "which He worked in Christ when He raised Him from the dead and seated Him at His right hand in the heavenly places, far above all principality and power and might and dominion, and every name that is named, not only in this age but also in that which is to come. And He put all things under His feet and gave Him to be head over all things to the church." This passage makes it clear that Jesus is far above all principalities, and because we are in Him, we share in His authority.

Furthermore, Ephesians 2:6 (NKJV) states, "and raised us up together, and made us sit together in the heavenly places in Christ Jesus." This means that believers are seated with Christ in heavenly places, positioned above every demonic structure. Many misunderstand spiritual warfare, believing that territorial spirits own and rule over certain locations, but this is not the case. While demons may abide in specific places, they do not have dominion over them. Psalm 115:16 (NKJV) affirms, "The heaven, even the heavens, are the Lord's; but the earth He has given to the children of men." God has entrusted dominion over the earth to mankind, meaning that it is the responsibility of believers to exercise spiritual authority over regions, cities, and territories.

Jesus Himself gives us insight into the territorial nature of demonic spirits. In Mark 5:10 (NKJV), after Jesus cast out the legion of demons from the possessed man, "they begged Him earnestly that He would not send them out of the country." This reveals that demons prefer certain territories, likely due to strongholds and spiritual climates conducive to their influence. However, their presence in a place does not mean ownership. They remain in locations only when unchallenged, but as believers, we have full authority in Christ to cast them out. Ephesians 1:22 (NKJV) reminds us that "He put all things under His feet and gave Him to be head over all things to the church." If all things are under Jesus' feet, and we are seated with Him, then principalities are under our feet as well.

When believers pray over cities and locales, they are not engaging in a battle from below, trying to defeat demonic rulers above them. Instead, they are declaring victory from a position of authority in Christ who is seated above demonic rulers, enforcing what Jesus has already won. Spiritual warfare is not about pleading for victory but about exercising the dominion that has been granted through Christ. This is why Jesus instructs believers in Luke 10:19 (NKJV), "Behold, I give you the authority to trample on serpents and scorpions, and over all the power of the enemy, and nothing shall by any means hurt you."

Have you ever been to a city, walked into a room, or stood next to a person and felt a dark, heavy, demonic presence? You start to feel uncomfortable. The question is: why do you feel that way when you have the power of God working in you and through you? If anything, whenever you walk into a room, all those demons should feel uncomfortable because the light has come.

As believers, we must recognize the weaponry at our disposal. We have the Name of Jesus, angels, the Holy Spirit, Jesus Himself, and the Omnipotent God working on our behalf. When the devil looks at you, he is not afraid of you—he is afraid of the One standing behind you.

We have been falsely taught in many church circles about the power of darkness and the discernment of spirits. We have Christians who can discern the demonic activity in a room but cannot discern the power of God working behind the scenes to cleanse it. It is time for Christians to wake up and stop with all this foolishness. Walk in your authority! Whenever you walk into a place, those massive angels are going before you to clear the way.

This is not an Old Testament-style battle where angels struggle against other angels. In fact, there is no fight at all. You walk in, and the demons leave. You have the authority. If the demons stay, it is because God allows them to stay to accomplish His purpose. But even then, if you ask your Father God to remove them, they will be removed in an instant.

Now, this is not to say that things with the people involved will return to normal. In fact, if those demons have trained the people to act foolishly, they will continue to do so long after the demons are gone because those individuals need to be transformed by the renewing of their minds in Christ. Otherwise, they will default to the behaviors they learned from the devil.

This does not mean they are possessed! It means they were trained, like dogs, to behave a certain way. And to be honest, as stated earlier in this teaching, all of us at some point have been trained by the devil, which is why we struggle with certain sins and behaviors.

Keep in mind after knowing all of this, be mindful that demons may resist leaving territories, but they have no legal right to remain when confronted by a believer operating in the authority of Jesus Christ. Through prayer, declaration, and faith in the finished work of Christ, believers can overthrow spiritual strongholds and proclaim territories for the Kingdom of God. The principalities are not above us—we are above them, seated with Christ Jesus in heavenly places, with all authority to enforce His victory on the earth. Remember, it all belongs to God.

Chapter 9

Images of Satan and Demons: Truth vs. Lies

We have all seen movies and artistic depictions of Satan and his demonic cohorts, but have you ever questioned whether these images are accurate? A few essential questions to ask are: Where did man get these images of Satan? What does the Bible actually say about his appearance? Are demons truly hideous in form? Many assume that these depictions are biblical, but a closer examination reveals otherwise.

A study of historical art and religious influence points to one primary source for our modern images of Satan—the early Catholic Church. Nearly all commonly accepted portrayals of Satan and demons have been shaped by Catholic iconography rather than by Scripture. While other cultures and religions have depicted grotesque creatures, it is important to distinguish truth from myth. As followers of Christ, we are called to live in truth and remove falsehoods from our understanding. John 8:32 (NKJV) states, *"And you shall know the truth, and the truth shall make you free."* If our perception of Satan is based on artistic tradition rather than Scripture, then we must reevaluate what we believe.

Some of the most common images of Satan and demons include:

- Dark and shadowy figures with glowing red eyes
- Red with fangs, tails, hooves, and pitchforks
- A goat-like entity
- A being with horns and cat-like eyes

- Bat-like wings

- Half-animal, half-human hybrids

However, nowhere in the Bible is Satan described as a monstrous figure. The verses often cited to justify his grotesque appearance do not support this idea. Revelation 12:9 (NKJV) states, *"So the great dragon was cast out, that serpent of old, called the Devil and Satan, who deceives the whole world; he was cast to the earth, and his angels were cast out with him."* Many assume that the terms "dragon" and "serpent" refer to his physical appearance, but these are symbolic descriptions of his deceptive and destructive nature. Throughout biblical history, Satan is often referred to as "that old serpent" because he took on the form of a serpent in the Garden of Eden (Genesis 3:1-5). This, however, does not indicate his true form but rather his ability to masquerade in different ways.

In fact, the Bible presents the opposite of the commonly held image of Satan. 2 Corinthians 11:14 (NKJV) states, *"And no wonder! For Satan himself transforms himself into an angel of light."* Rather than being a hideous monster, Satan is capable of appearing as something appealing and beautiful, which aligns with his deceptive nature. His power lies not in fearsome appearance but in deception. Likewise, Isaiah 14:16 (NKJV) provides insight into how Satan will ultimately be viewed: *"Those who see you will gaze at you, and consider you, saying: 'Is this the man who made the earth tremble, who shook kingdoms?'"* This verse suggests that Satan's true form will not be terrifying but underwhelming, causing people to marvel at how such a being could have had so much influence.

The biblical reality is that Satan and demons are not monstrous figures lurking in the shadows but rather spiritual entities that manipulate, deceive, and masquerade as light. Satan's greatest weapon is not his appearance but his ability to lead people away from the truth. Therefore, believers must base their understanding on Scripture, not on myths, religious tradition, or artistic interpretations. Colossians 2:8 (NKJV) warns, *"Beware lest anyone cheat you through philosophy and empty deceit, according to the tradition of men, according to the basic principles of the world, and not according to Christ."* We must remain grounded in biblical truth, recognizing that Satan's influence is found in deception, not in terrifying imagery.

Chapter 10

The responsibility of the believer

It is the ultimate responsibility of the believer to put their entire faith, hope, and trust in Jesus. Because if you don't, you will end up exhausting yourself by engaging in endless and mindless spiritual battles that you are simply not capable of winning—nor do you have the endurance to win. Remember, spirits don't need rest. Humans do. The war is waging every day, 24 hours a day, nonstop. You cannot live your life warring every day.

The authority of the believer does not rest or rely on what an individual does to live holy. It all rests upon Christ, His power, and His abilities. Because if we base it upon our ability to live a sinless life, then none of us would have the right to cast out demons or engage in spiritual warfare.

The question arises: does this mean that a Christian can live in sin and still cast out demons? Well, this answer is a bit challenging because it still assumes that the power to cast out demons rests solely upon the believer's efforts and not upon the finished work of Christ. But does this mean God is okay with a person living in sin? No.

What we need to understand as believers is that only God knows the heart of a man; we only see the outward. So if, in your heart, you feel that because of your sin you should not cast out a demon, then the Bible says in Romans 14, "Anything not done in faith is sin. He who doubts is condemned." Thus, even if you did attempt to cast out demons, nothing would happen unless God intervened. But isn't that how it works anyway?

What about the belief that only certain people are gifted to cast out demons? There is a belief that casting out demons and engaging in certain supernatural activities is a special calling that not everyone is meant to do. I have even heard teachers claim that if a person is not called to deliverance ministry, they should not engage in it but rather call on someone who is specifically called to that ministry.

There are two problems with this belief. First, it is unbiblical. There is no mention in the Bible of "deliverance ministry" as an official ministry. The Bible explicitly lists the ministries in 1 Corinthians 12:5-10: "There are differences of ministries, but the same Lord. And there are diversities of activities, but it is the same God who works all in all. But the manifestation of the Spirit is given to each one for the profit of all: for to one is given the word of wisdom through the Spirit, to another the word of knowledge through the same Spirit, to another faith by the same Spirit, to another gifts of healings by the same Spirit, to another the working of miracles, to another prophecy, to another discerning of spirits, to another different kinds of tongues, to another the interpretation of tongues." Did you notice that "deliverance" was not listed as one of the ministries in Scripture?

Second, the Bible grants authority to all believers, not just a select few. However, Jesus admonishes each believer in Luke 10:20: "Nevertheless, do not rejoice in this, that the spirits are subject to you, but rather rejoice because your names are written in heaven." We have been given authority, but we are not to rejoice or boast in this authority because it is not by our own efforts that we have this ability—it is given by God Himself.

Chapter 11

Historical Precedence of Demonic Activity Post Ascension

There are numerous accounts in early church history of various demonic activities within a community of believers. In this section, we will provide a more biblical alternative explanation of those events based on our current understanding of the situation. We will examine two major events: the first will focus on post-ascension demonic activity as recorded in the Bible, and the second will explore demonic activity documented by early church historians.

First, we will discuss post-ascension demonic activity as recorded in the Bible. In Acts 16, we read about an encounter that the Apostle Paul had with a young girl who had a spirit of divination. Verse 16 states, "Now it happened, as we went to prayer, that a certain slave girl possessed with a spirit of divination met us, who brought her masters much profit by fortune-telling." This is the first time since the ascension of Christ that a spirit is mentioned by name. Traditional scholars state that this was not the actual name of the demon, but rather that Paul was calling out the demon's behavior. However, there is a better explanation for this event.

During this time, one of the most well-known religious cults was the Oracle of Delphi, where priestesses, known as the Pythia, served as mediums for the god Apollo. These women would enter caves and inhale intoxicating volcanic fumes rising from fissures in the earth, causing them to enter a trancelike state. In this altered state, they would make prophetic utterances, which were highly revered and interpreted by male priests, influencing political and military decisions across the Greco-Roman world.

So, the question arises: was this truly a demonic spirit? The answer lies within the honesty of Luke's discourse, where he provides a subtle hint as to what he thought was really happening. He states in Acts 16:18, "But Paul, greatly annoyed, turned and said to the spirit, 'I command you in the name of Jesus Christ to come out of her.' And he came out that very hour."

Did anything in this verse stand out? Luke wrote, "that very hour." Does this imply that it took a demon a full hour to leave? Or is there something else at play here? Consider this: in previous encounters with demons, they departed immediately when confronted. However, in instances where healings took place, many accounts state something similar—"within that very hour." So, was this deliverance or healing? Without modern knowledge of how intoxication works, it is reasonable to assume that this was a healing—or rather, a detoxification.

The key point to recognize here is that it does not really matter whether this was a demon or not. Paul believed it was a demon. Luke described it as healing through detoxification. However, regardless of one's perspective, the most important takeaway is this: when the name of Jesus is invoked, the power of God is not dependent on human understanding of the situation! Remember, we serve an omnipotent and omniscient God. He is never unaware—He knows exactly what is happening. He understands the intent behind the command. Stop putting limits on God's ability. Simply do your part, and He will do His.

Now that we have looked at post-ascension demonic activity as recorded in the Bible, let's now explore demonic activity documented by early church historians of Scripture.

Let's look at one of the more prolific church fathers, St. Augustine. Many teachers within the charismatic movement quote him as saying that Christians can be demon-possessed. This is simply not true. In his treatise, City of God, he acknowledged that demons could torment the righteous, but he did not teach that a Christian could be possessed. In fact, none of the early church fathers explicitly stated that a Christian could be demon-possessed. They did mention that Christians could be afflicted, but that is precisely what the Bible says—this is not a new concept.

As we look deeper into church history especially in the 1600s, we note the Salem witch trials and an entire period of documentation of demonic activity. Because of their lack of scientific knowledge, the people of Salem Village in 1692 believed that strange and frightening behaviors were caused by witchcraft and demonic activity. The Puritans were deeply religious and thought that Satan used witches to harm their community. When young girls began experiencing seizures, hallucinations, muscle spasms, and sensations of being choked or pinched, many assumed they were under attack by witches. These girls claimed to see ghostly figures, demonic apparitions, and spirits of accused witches tormenting them, leading to widespread panic and the infamous Salem witch trials (Caporael, 1976).

The crisis spread beyond Salem Village (now Danvers, Massachusetts) to Salem Town, Andover, and Boston, where accused individuals were held in prison (Caporael, 1976). It started in late 1691, with reports of unexplained afflictions.

What the people of Salem did not realize was that these symptoms were not supernatural, but rather the result of ergot poisoning. Ergot is a toxic fungus (Claviceps purpurea) that infects rye, a grain commonly eaten by the Puritans. When consumed, it causes convulsions, hallucinations, muscle contractions, vomiting, and a sensation of bugs crawling under the skin. The weather in 1691-1692 created ideal conditions for ergot to grow—warm, damp, and rainy springs followed by humid summers. Since rye was harvested in August and stored for months before consumption, people likely began experiencing poisoning symptoms in the winter, which aligned with the first reports of afflictions in Salem (Caporael, 1976).

Similar incidents occurred in Europe before and after Salem. In France (17th century), particularly in the region of Lorraine, outbreaks of convulsive ergotism caused symptoms that were mistaken for demonic possession, leading to witch hunts and executions. In Germany, the region of Saxony saw clergy debates in the 1700s over whether ergot poisoning or demonic possession caused mass hysteria and convulsions. Even in England, in the early 1600s, a woman named Alice Trevisard was accused of witchcraft after her hands and feet "rotted away," which was likely gangrenous ergotism. A similar case in 1762 saw an English family suffer from ergot poisoning, but the head of the household blamed it on witchcraft, reflecting the persistent superstition surrounding the disease (Caporael, 1976).

The Salem witch trials and similar European cases show how a lack of medical understanding, combined with religious fears and social tensions, led to wrongful accusations and executions. These events stand as a historical warning of how ignorance and fear can escalate into tragedy. This is why, before taking historical records into account, it is important to remember that their explanations of events may not be based on factual knowledge but rather on anecdotal misinformation.

Chapter 12

Skepticism

Many followers of traditional charismatic teachings on the supernatural might find this book challenging because their personal experiences seem to contradict its content. Over the years, I've met many people from various countries who insist that their firsthand experiences prove demons can physically manipulate the natural world.

For instance, numerous missionaries and Christians have reported seeing demons cause objects to levitate or fly across rooms. While I listen respectfully to these accounts, I often find myself questioning their validity. For example, if a demon has the power to throw an object, why doesn't it aim directly at people? If Satan's aim is to kill, steal, and destroy, why hasn't he used this power to cause direct harm? Moreover, why do these occurrences happen so infrequently?

When logically analyzed, these accounts often raise more questions than they answer. This is why it's essential to evaluate supernatural claims in light of Scripture rather than relying solely on personal experience.

Another factor that made me skeptical about people's supernatural claims was the absence of any notable change in their lives following such experiences. Scripture shows us that genuine supernatural encounters, like those of Moses in the Old Testament and Paul in the New Testament, lead to profound transformations in character and behavior. Moses went from being a timid man to a confident leader after his encounter with God, despite having fled after killing an Egyptian and hiding for 40 years. Similarly, Paul transformed from a persecutor of Christians to a devoted follower of Christ willing to die for the gospel. However, when I look at those who share their supernatural experiences, I often don't see any significant change in their behavior or character; they continue living as they did before their supposed encounters.

Think about it—if you genuinely encounter a supernatural entity, wouldn't that experience be proof enough that God is real? And wouldn't such an encounter naturally lead to significant personal change?

Driven by my growing skepticism, I decided to test the validity of these supernatural claims myself. I chose to go to Haiti, known as a hotspot for demonic activity in the northern hemisphere, to see if I could personally experience the supernatural. I told myself that this trip would confirm whether or not the supernatural—and indeed God Himself—is real. I didn't want to follow a God who couldn't stand up to the devil, nor did I want to remain in uncertainty. So, I intentionally broke a charismatic rule and went looking for a confrontation, a real test of my faith.

As I traveled from village to village asking for voodoo doctors, they were mysteriously absent wherever I went. At night, I stayed awake, hoping to witness some form of supernatural activity, but nothing happened. I slept better in Haiti than I had back in America. The only close encounter involved a woman said to be demon-possessed, who bit a pastor during an exorcism. However, seeing her calm and happy in church later made me question if her issues were more psychological than demonic.

From these experiences, I learned that not all mental health issues are linked to demonic activity and vice versa. Regardless of the nature of the problem, invoking the name of Jesus and allowing Christ to intervene is always the appropriate response.

The question often arises: what could be the cause of people sharing so many similar testimonies about supernatural experiences? Apart from dismissing these stories as pure delirium, I adopted a more pragmatic approach to investigate further. I spent time examining footage of witch doctors, voodoo practitioners, and other occult figures. A common element I observed was their use of incense or substances like candles, wood, or what they referred to as sage.

Reflecting on my own experiences, I remembered how my friends could get high from secondhand exposure without directly consuming drugs—simply by breathing in the air around them, they would eventually feel the effects. This led me to consider the possibility that those claiming to have witnessed supernatural events might actually have been victims of intoxicating fumes, leading to hallucinations. While this theory cannot be definitively proven, it is a critical consideration.

Moreover, many Christians have shared stories that align with accounts from former hippies about the hallucinogenic effects of a drug known as acid. I learned early on that acid can be absorbed through the skin from treated paper, causing euphoric and psychedelic effects. Therefore, when interacting with practitioners of the occult, it is wise to avoid touching any substances they offer, as these could potentially be drugs similar to acid.

In conclusion, while the true nature of these supernatural claims remains uncertain, it is prudent to approach such situations with caution. Whether the effects are due to drug exposure or other influences, the risk of drug intoxication is a genuine concern. Always remain vigilant and consider the possible physical explanations behind purported supernatural experiences, especially when they occur in environments controlled by occult practices.

Does this mean we should walk in fear of being drugged? Absolutely not! Jesus said in Mark 16:17-18 (NKJV), "And these signs will follow those who believe: In My name they will cast out demons; they will speak with new tongues; they will take up serpents; and if they drink anything deadly, it will by no means hurt them." This means that even if we are exposed, God will protect us. And whether the issue is demonic activity or drug-induced psychosis, invoking the name of Jesus in every situation remains the solution to the problem. Never forget that it is not our job to try to explain the supernatural. It is far too big for human comprehension. Our only job is to invoke the name of Jesus and allow Him to do His work.

Chapter 13

A Warning to the False Believer

This part of the book will serve as a warning to those who intend to walk in Christ's authority without first allowing Christ to be the authority over their lives. In order to walk in Christ's authority, you must be under His authority. You must willingly allow Him to be the Lord of your life.

In this modern era of Christianity, many people reading this book have been fed a false gospel, and regretfully, many of them are false believers. What is a false believer? The first mention of false believers is found in Galatians 2:4-5: "And this occurred because of false brethren (false believers) secretly brought in (who came in by stealth to spy out our liberty which we have in Christ Jesus, that they might bring us into bondage)." A false believer is someone who appears to be a follower of Christ but has not truly committed their life to Him. This type of person may go to church and participate in all the rituals, but their heart is far from God.

Jesus says in Matthew 15:8-9: "'These people draw near to Me with their mouth, and honor Me with their lips, but their heart is far from Me. And in vain they worship Me, teaching as doctrines the commandments of men.'" These types of people do not truly know God's Word. Rather, they know more about man-made theologies and human traditions than the Word of God itself. The sad thing about these individuals is that even when confronted with the Word of God, they are so blinded by human teachings that they cannot see the light of truth.

Sadly, this is the case with many teachers who focus on the supernatural. They do not lean on the foundation of Holy Scripture and instead lead people away from the grace of God into a works-based system, teaching that spiritual authority must be earned through rituals and works.

The teaching in the book is only for those who trust in the grace of God through Christ Jesus. I do not want you to fall into a works-based mentality. However, I also do not want people who are not fully surrendered to Jesus to have a false assurance that they will be able to walk in the authority mentioned in this book.

Remember, the demons know who belongs to God and who does not. The story of the sons of Sceva in Acts 19:14-16 illustrates this: "And the evil spirit answered and said, 'Jesus I know, and Paul I know; but who are you?'" The demons are fully aware of who belongs to Christ. So, if you are not confident in your relationship with Jesus, use this time to solidify your relationship, because the truths discussed in this book are real. And if they are real, then there will come a day when you will stand before God in judgment.

References

Caporael, L. R. (1976). Ergotism: The Satan loosed in Salem? Science, 192(4234), 21-26.

Augustine of Hippo, City of God, Book XIX, Chapter 13.

Made in United States
Orlando, FL
24 May 2025